To Martha –

A small token which conveys much love and all best wishes for happiness along the Road of Life. May this little book be some help or inspiration to you along that Road –

Margaret & Dick

May 30, 1956

I Thessalonians 1: 3
II Peter 3:18

THE
WHOLE
ARMOR OF
GOD

BOOKS BY RALPH W. SOCKMAN

THE WHOLE ARMOR OF GOD

HOW TO BELIEVE

THE HIGHER HAPPINESS

NOW TO LIVE!

THE FINE ART OF USING

THE LORD'S PRAYER

DATE WITH DESTINY

THE HIGHWAY OF GOD

LIVE FOR TOMORROW

RECOVERIES IN RELIGION

THE PARADOXES OF JESUS

THE UNEMPLOYED CARPENTER

MORALS OF TOMORROW

MEN OF THE MYSTERIES

SUBURBS OF CHRISTIANITY

THE REVIVAL OF THE CONVENTIONAL LIFE IN
THE CHURCH OF ENGLAND IN THE NINE-
TEENTH CENTURY (Thesis)

THE
WHOLE
ARMOR OF
GOD

Ralph W. Sockman

Abingdon Press

NEW YORK • NASHVILLE

THE WHOLE ARMOR OF GOD

Copyright MCMLV by Pierce & Washabaugh

Library of Congress Catalog Card Number: 55-6075

B

SET UP, PRINTED, AND BOUND BY THE
PARTHENON PRESS, AT NASHVILLE,
TENNESSEE, UNITED STATES OF AMERICA

To
my little granddaughter
LISA
who in two years has discovered
all the chinks in my armor

Foreword

In his sonnet "to a friend," matthew arnold paid the man this tribute:

> Be his
> My special thanks, whose even-balanc'd soul,
> .   .   .   .
> Business could not make dull, nor Passion wild:
> Who saw life steadily, and saw it whole.

Those words were high praise in Arnold's day a century ago, and they would be an even higher tribute today. We live in a society of increasing specialization. We immerse ourselves in our own occupations in order to get ahead. Thus we come to know our own lines, but often we become too busy to lift our eyes to the general patterns of living. The result of such specialization is, as Alfred Noyes has said, that we are misled by small clever minds, that is, minds which know their own field but not life in general.

One of the high functions of religion is to lift us out of our littleness and broaden us out of our narrowness that we may see "life steadily, and [see] it whole." Many persons have the mistaken idea that to be religious is to restrict the joys of living rather than to release the powers of life. Others think of religious activities as social extras, things people may do if they like that sort of thing, but hardly vital enough for busy, practical persons like themselves.

Religion involves the whole life of man in relation to God. One of the deplorable trends of our time is that many interpreters of religion run off on tangents. Some find it popular and profitable to specialize on the promises of God and interpret faith as a formula for peace of mind and earthly success. Others see Christ only as the crusader for social reform. Still others are prophets of doom stressing only the predictions of Christ's second coming. But "if salt has lost its taste, how can its saltness be restored," and if religion has lost its wholeness, how can we be made whole?

According to General Jan Smuts, "the creation of wholes and of wholeness generally is the inherent characteristic of the universe." Our departmentalized living needs to recover the wholeness of life. Hence we turn to look with the apostle Paul at the "whole armor of God."

Several valued friends have assisted in the preparation of this little book. I would express my gratitude to Miss Marion M. Marcy, Miss Dell Thomas, Miss Beatrice Meylan, Mrs. Helen Stanbury, Miss Vivian Bartlett, Mrs. W. C. Stevens, and to my wife, Zellah Endly Sockman.

RALPH W. SOCKMAN

Contents

I

The Whole Armor of God 11

II

The Girdle of Truth 21

III

The Breastplate of Righteousness 31

IV

The Sandals of Peace 40

V

The Shield of Faith 49

VI

The Helmet of Hope 59

VII

The Sword of the Spirit 69

"Therefore take the whole armor of God, that you may be able to withstand in the evil day, and having done all, to stand. Stand therefore, having girded your loins with truth, and having put on the breastplate of righteousness, and having shod your feet with the equipment of the gospel of peace; above all taking the shield of faith, with which you can quench all the flaming darts of the evil one. And take the helmet of salvation, and the sword of the Spirit, which is the word of God."

—Ephesians 6:13-17

CHAPTER I

The Whole Armor of God

SOME TIME AGO I SPENT A FEW VERY INTERESTING hours viewing exhibits of England's military history. In a London museum not far from the gate of the changing guards are preserved armor and weapons used in Britain's wars from the Battle of Hastings in the eleventh century to the Battle of the Bulge in World War II.

It is hard for the modern man in this day of submarines and atomic and hydrogen bombs to think his way back to the time when men fought with arrows and protected themselves with breastplates and shields. Those battles of the Middle Ages look to us like the bouts of little boys in a back alley. The ancient methods of fighting would tempt us to laughter were we not sobered by the tragic fact that while men have outgrown their primitive weapons, they have not outgrown the will to war. It is not the spread of peace but the improved destructiveness of war which has made ancient armor into museum pieces.

When we turn to the Bible and read the apostle Paul's description of what he calls "the whole armor of God," it may seem too out-of-date to be of interest. What help to us is all the apostle's talk about the breastplates and helmets and shields? Are such weapons any good against fears and anxieties and inferiority complexes and bodily ills and Communist propaganda, which we look upon as our chief dangers? Why not leave those weapons of the early Christians as museum pieces and get on with the real business of religion, which

11

is to protect our peace of mind from worries, our bodies from pain, and our society from Communism?

No doubt that is the way many people look at it. But it is my conviction that the Bible is not yet outgrown and that we need to get back to the springs of our faith in order to keep the streams of our thinking pure. Also it is my desire to preach the whole gospel. It is not right to promote some one aspect of religion to the neglect of other phases of biblical teaching.

Hence I shall devote these chapters to the injunction given by the apostle Paul in the sixth chapter of Ephesians: "Therefore take the whole armor of God, that you may be able to withstand in the evil day, and having done all, to stand." We shall try to see the realities symbolized in such expressions as "the breastplate of righteousness" and "the shield of faith." I begin with my reasons for considering the theme "the whole armor of God."

The first reason is that it may reawaken us to the *wholeness of our Christian faith*. When we read the Gospels in the King James Version, we are struck by the frequent repetition of the word "whole." Again and again we read that Jesus touched the sick and they were made "whole." The Revised Standard Version usually translates the word differently. For instance, the King James Version records Jesus as asking the ill man at the pool of Bethesda, "Wilt thou be made whole?" But the Revised Version expresses it thus, "Do you want to be healed?" And again, when the Pharisees criticized Jesus for dining with sinners and publicans, he replied, "They that are whole have no need of the physician." But the Revised Version's translation is, "Those who are well have no need of a physician."

Now while in general I greatly respect the accuracy of the Revised Standard Version, I wonder if the words "healed" and "well" quite fully express all that Jesus meant

12

by the word "whole." I believe the Master meant by "wholeness" something more than mere "wellness," if I may coin a word. When we say, "I feel well," we mean that we have no aches or pains; we have a good appetite; we feel fit. But we may feel well and yet not be whole. I think of a man who is pretty nearly a perfect physical specimen. He is never sick. He is able to eat what he likes and do pretty much what he pleases. He feels well. But he certainly is not living a whole, full life as his Creator intended. He is merely self-contained in too small a container.

Christ came to reveal a wholeness of life which even such well-feeling persons miss. One of the weaknesses of some popular religion today is that it aims to make people feel good rather than to be good. Jesus said, "I came that they may have life, and have it abundantly."

Christ brings these enlarging lives of ours into harmonious wholeness by helping us to integrate ourselves. The classic formula for self-integration is commonly regarded as that which Shakespeare gave in Hamlet:

> To thine own self be true,
> And it must follow, as the night the day,
> Thou canst not then be false to any man.

Those words, as you recall, were spoken by Polonius to young Laertes. But suppose Polonius had given that advice to Hamlet himself. Would the distraught young Dane have understood what it meant to be true to himself? Ah—no. He was not himself. He was beside himself. It is not enough merely to say, "Be true to yourself." A man needs to be shown what his true self is. And it is this double service which Christ renders. He helps us to be true to ourselves and shows us what is our true selfhood.

13

The second reason for considering "the whole armor of God" is that it may reawaken us to the *"heroic aspects of our Christian faith."* Consider the situation of those early Christians to whom the command was given. Even if we accept this letter to the Ephesians as a general epistle rather than as one written specifically to the converts in the city of Ephesus, nevertheless for the sake of their faith they had done one of the hardest things which we human beings are called upon to do. They had cut themselves off from their old social attachments. They had forfeited dear and vital friendships. They had to struggle against the pull of their old pagan associations, intensified by family feelings. There was the social stigma attached to membership in this new Christian sect.

In a day when church membership is regarded as a badge of social acceptability, it is hard to picture the price which early Christians paid for their faith. When I think of Christ's first followers, some very searching questions come home to me. Would I join the church if it meant cutting myself off from my family and friends? Would I line up with the Christians if they were looked down upon socially as outcasts? Would I call myself a Christian if that label closed the doors of business opportunities?

When we compare the sacrifices of the early Christians with our own, we see how soft and easy we have made religion. Dean Inge of St. Paul's, London, was a man of piercing intellect and mordant wit. He realized the contrast between the heroism of Christ's first followers and the softness of our comfort-seeking churches. He suggested that a change should be made in a certain familiar hymn. The hymn goes like this:

> They climbed the steep ascent of heav'n,
>> Thro' peril, toil, and pain:
> O God, to us may grace be given
>> To follow *in* their train!

Dean Inge's suggestion is that the last lines of the stanza should read:

> O God, to us may grace be given
> To follow *by* the train.

Yes, we follow by Pullman where the pioneer saints trod with blood and sweat and tears.

There is such obvious irony in likening conventional modern churchmen with the early soldiers of Christ that we are loath to sing the old crusading hymns of the church. As a lad I was stirred by the strains of "Onward, Christian Soldiers." But now I see the difficulty of singing:

> Like a mighty army
> Moves the Church of God;
> Brothers, we are treading
> Where the saints have trod.

You see, we do not try to recruit members for the church as if they were enlisting in an army. Whereas the early Christians heard the call of Christ as the summons of a commander to battle, the popular trend of our day is to invite men to church as a salesman calls to a bargain. We think the church will appeal to people more if we stress what it *offers* rather than what it *requires*. Whereas the early Christians in joining the church had to leave friends and endure loneliness, we try to persuade people to come to church in order to find congenial friends. Whereas the first followers of Christ often had to forfeit business opportunities, some pulpits now proclaim that to follow Christ will mean financial success. Prayer is often advocated as the way to get what you want of this world's goods. As has been said, the tendency of the modern church is to take out the cross and put in cushions.

In the first two or three centuries after Christ the

15

Christian church was the danger zone of society. Secular living was quite safe under the Caesars. It was by joining the church that a person incurred risk of persecution and even death. But in our day we woo people to the church by telling them it is the place to escape fear and anxiety and all the other "shocks that flesh is heir to."

Well, let us be honest with ourselves. Life is hard enough at best, we say. Why make it harder? We have enough burdens to bear. Why tell us that the early Christians were more heroic than we? What we want is a lift for our loads and security for our lives.

Yes, I grant all that. But still there are one or two questions that will not down. When I see the price which the early Christians were willing to pay for their faith, I wonder if they found some values in it which we are missing. Maybe they risked more and sacrificed more because they discovered more of "the unsearchable riches of Christ." Maybe we want to get our religion cheaply because we are missing its real values.

And then the other question that disturbs me is this: Am I getting spiritually soft? Am I losing something of the tough fiber which it takes to be a true Christian?

When I think of the bravery displayed by our soldiers under Communist brain washing, and when I consider what the early Christians endured under their persecution, my head is bowed in humility at my own lack of courage, but my heart rises in response to the heroism of others.

The third reason for considering the armor of God is that it may awaken us to the *responsibility* as well as the wholeness and heroism of our faith.

The words "safety" and "salvation" stem from the same root, but they produce different fruit. Some time ago I asked my closest adviser what is the difference between safety and salvation. She answered that safety suggests being saved *from* something and salvation suggests being saved *for* something.

That distinction has much truth in it. And we should pause a moment to ask ourselves what is our primary concern in religion, to be kept safe from harm in this world and the next, or to be saved for the good we can do in this world and the next.

Here again let us be realistic enough to admit that we do have a concern for our own security. We want to be saved from disasters and dictators and disease and Communism, from the evils others may do to us and from the consequences of our own sins. Nevertheless not merely is the armor of God meant for our own protection, but it is to equip us to fulfill our duties as soldiers of Christ responsible for others. Men and women do not join the army of our country for the sake of their own safety, but for the service of the nation. Likewise men put on the armor of God for the service of their Lord.

A Christian dons his armor because he feels responsible for the welfare of those closest to him. A person could not call himself a Christian if he was not concerned about the physical and spiritual welfare of his family. As a boy I was fascinated by the stories and pictures of Indians lurking around to attack the homes of the early American settlers. The old frontier dangers are gone. But our homes are still threatened by invasions of vice and vulgarity, by worldliness and selfishness, which disrupt families. I was greatly heartened in a suburban community to learn how many young fathers and mothers were being recruited to teach church-school classes on Sunday mornings. They form the valued company of home guards. And I think of the mothers who make lives in the home while we men are trying to make money in the market place. No man in uniform is doing more to defend our country than the homemakers who wear the armor of God.

A Christian also feels responsible for the church. When

17

I go into my pulpit, I am confident that there are hundreds of persons praying for me. At the door of many an English church I have seen this sign: "Let those who enter pray for those who worship and minister here." George Bernard Shaw once likened a modern church congregation to a mob of hermits coming with their cups to a well of water to fill them and carry them back to their caves. If that is the way people go to church, they are not going as Christians. A Christian congregation is a fellowship of the responsible. Just as men join the army not for their health but for service, so good people join the church for service not for their health.

A follower of Christ also feels responsible for his nation. If an American citizen gets into trouble when abroad, he expects his government to assume some responsibility for him. But we must also remember that we are responsible *for* our government. J. B. Priestly once said: "We should behave toward our country as women behave toward the men they love. A loving wife will do anything for her husband except stop criticizing and trying to improve him." Perhaps we should pause here to let that sink in! But to go on with Priestley: "We should cast the same affectionate but sharp glance at our country. We should love it but also insist on telling it all its faults. The noisy, empty patriot, not the critic, is the dangerous citizen."

We, as loyal citizens, are responsible *to* our government. But as Christians we are also responsible to God *for* our government. In time of war it is assumed that patriotic citizens will defend their nation's honor. But in time of peace it should also be assumed that Christian citizens will fight to make their nation's honor worthy to be defended. Jesus said, "I have not come to bring peace, but a sword." As I understand him, Jesus did not mean that he came to bring the physical sword of war. He meant that he came to call followers to be soldiers of peace, persons who will be as heroic and sacrificial in the work of peace as soldiers are in battle.

How are we to preserve the precious freedoms which our Western world enjoys? Not by fighting dictators abroad. We have done that in two world wars, and now we are told that we face a more sinister danger in Communism than we confronted in the Kaiser and in Hitler. We must fight the evils which are threatening our welfare at home, such as crime and corruption, time-killing and money-wasting practices in public and private work, pride and prejudice, selfishness, greed, and their like. And we shall do this not so much by public hearings in Washington as by private doings in our own communities. I pray that we may give less attention to the charges and countercharges of politicians and get ahead with our personal responsibilities as private citizens.

Being a Christian was once heroic business. It is yet if we live up to it. Being a Christian was once responsible business; it is yet. To put on the armor of God means enlisting for service.

A newspaper carried a picture of the mayor of New York swearing in a general to be in charge of our civil defense. It is a nonsalaried position. Why did the mayor require him to take an oath? Why did he not just shake hands with the general and say, "Go to it"? Because high duties call for divine dedication. And so do ours.

A vow made unto the Lord serves to reinforce the human will. We are not always at our best. Knowing the weakness of our wills in face of irking or shattering temptations, we do well in moments of moral insight to pledge ourselves to the side of goodness with the help of God. That is why the Psalmist said, "I will pay my vows to the Lord in the presence of all his people."

We are not all visible to one another, but we are all

visible to God. So with the eye of God upon us, let us join in a vow to put on the whole armor of God.

PRAYER:

Our Father, in whose love we have our hope and in whose strength we bear our burdens, grant us the sense of thy nearness. May we feel so close to thee, whom we cannot see, that we may be near in spirit to others, for we are all thy children, members of thy one great family. By thy wisdom save us from false choices and futile fears. Through thy love make us humble enough to be forgiven and gracious enough to forgive. So fill us with confidence in thee that we shall impart courage to those we meet. Comfort those who face pain and adversity that they may have faith and fortitude. Day by day may we grow in purity and power, in sympathy and understanding. And then, O God, mingle us at last with the mighty host of thy redeemed. We ask through Jesus Christ our Lord. Amen.

CHAPTER II

The Girdle of Truth

THE FIRST EQUIPMENT IN THE ARMOR OF GOD which the apostle Paul mentions is the girdle of truth. "Stand therefore, having girded your loins with truth."

A strong belt or girdle was a necessary part of ordinary civilian attire in the lands of the Near East. Without such a girding, the loose, flowing garments became cumbersome, flapping about the limbs and hindering the movement of the body. And in the uniform of the soldier the belt was still more imperative. It held the various pieces of armor securely in place. Loose armor left the wearer uncomfortable and unsafe. Without the girdle the soldier would feel that he was going to pieces.

The first century could see the force of Paul's figure of speech. But what significance has it for us?

The first question we ask is: *"What is it to gird one's loins with truth?"*

For one thing, it is to have a mind which seeks the truth. And we must remember that seeking truth is more than finding facts. Many people try to secure facts to prove that they are right rather than to discover the truth and learn what is right. We see this so often in political and religious controversies.

But to have your loins girt with truth means that your single-eyed aim is to find out what is true, cost what it may, lead where it will. Truth is basic to all other considerations. The person who tries to be righteous without first seeking truth may become a bigot. The man who has courage without truthfulness may become dangerous. The person who cherishes hopes without seeking truth becomes an idle dreamer. We cannot build a sound faith on false beliefs. We cannot build sound national security on false charges. We must be earnest to seek the truth and honest to follow where it leads.

And note that this means more than merely being sincere. The Puritans of Massachusetts Bay, when they drove out Roger Williams, were no doubt sincere in believing they were right and he was wrong. The Spanish Inquisitors in the sixteenth century were many of them sincere when they burned heretics at the stake. Undoubtedly many in the Jerusalem crowd which called for Jesus' crucifixion were sincere in believing that he was a malefactor.

The soldier who puts on the armor of God must do more than fight to defend the truth as he sees it. He must fight to find out the truth. He must overcome the inertia of his own mind which would leave him content with rumors and appearances. He must struggle against his pride, which clings to his preconceived ideas and prejudices and makes him unwilling to re-examine his views and change his opinions.

To have one's loins girt with truth is to have one's whole nature held together by integrity. This integrity shows itself in small matters as well as in great. It is manifest in the courtroom where a person refuses to perjure himself and also in business and social circles where he refuses to compromise himself. The man of integrity hates untruth as untruth. He detests false pretenses in religion and "stuffed shirts" wherever found. He is pained by painted wood which is meant to pass for marble and by gilding which would deceive the eye as gold.

Ralph Adams Cram, the late great architect, was wont to say that the exterior of a church should be secondary to

22

its interior. All too often church builders put up an imposing front to impress the passer-by and then economize by cheapening the furnishings within. But, said Dr. Cram, a church should be like a Christian in that it gets better and richer the farther in you go.

Such a statement is in line with our Lord's teaching. Jesus rebuked the pretentious Pharisees who cleansed the outside of the cup and left the inside, as he said, full of dead men's bones. He called such hypocrites "whited sepulchres." Christ bade his followers look first to the quality of the inner life, asserting that what was hidden would eventually be revealed.

In *The Bridge of San Luis Rey,* Thornton Wilder portrayed a wise and talented music teacher, Uncle Pio, who discovered a young singer in South America. The girl had much promise, but she was content to please the second-rate taste of music-hall crowds. Every night after basking in the popular applause, she found Uncle Pio waiting in the wings. The salvos from the stalls did not satisfy him. His true musicianship demanded her best.

So with us. The crowd's applause does not prove our greatness. The Master of the world is always waiting in the wings to see whether we ring true.

In short, to have your loins girt with truth is not only to be a seeker of truth and a speaker of truth, but to be a true person.

The second question one asks is: *"How do we gird our loins with truth?"* If to be girt with truth means this inner core of integrity, as I have tried to show, then it follows that it cannot be put on externally and quickly. We cannot live loosely and falsely six days a week and then be true on Sundays. We cannot snap into truthfulness in an emergency. That truth is as old as Aesop.

A certain little girl I know likes jokes. She likes to

hear them, and she likes to play them. Her grandfather, whom I also know pretty well, took it upon himself to explain to her the difference between statements made in fun and those made seriously. He told her Aesop's fable "The Shepherd's Boy." One day the boy, who was out watching the sheep, thought to have some fun and cried, "Wolf, Wolf!" The villagers came running only to find no wolf. Some days later the lad tried the same trick, and again his neighbors came to his help. Shortly afterward a wolf did attack the sheep, and the boy cried frantically for help. But this time the people thought he was fooling them again, and nobody came. The copybook maxim which accompanied the fable in the old school reader was this:

> The truth itself is not believed
> From one who often has deceived.

Aesop's own comment was: "A liar will not be believed, even when he speaks the truth."

That old fable has fresh warrant for arresting our attention today. We are desperately trying to detect disloyalty in all circles of society and government. Toward that end we have congressional investigations and court trials. But even though truth may be discovered by investigators, they cannot inculcate truthfulness.

We do not make people truthful merely by requiring them to take oaths in court. What force does an oath have on the mind of a Communist who does not believe in God? Truthfulness is a thing of habit rather than will. We have to live our way into truth.

We may be inclined to suspect persons who hide behind the Fifth Amendment. We ought also to be concerned about those who hide behind the modern "Eleventh Commandment." Some years ago a British novelist depicted a charac-

24

ter of whom he said that she had no regard for the Ten Commandments, but that she did have concern for an Eleventh
Commandment, which is, "Thou shalt not be found out."
A person who avoids falsehood and evil only through fear of
being found out is a "bad risk," whether in government or
business or the family or anywhere else.

We do not develop truthful people merely by multi-
plying detectives and trials. One disturbing feature of our
day is that so many people are not sufficiently sensitive to
truth to detect false notes and condemn charlatans and demagogues. We need a revival of genuineness and truthfulness
all the way from politics to religion.

And this can come only through a schooling of ourselves in truth. We must cultivate the love of truth until
false things repel us. Paul pointed the way when he wrote:
"Whatever is true, whatever is honorable, whatever is just,
whatever is pure, whatever is lovely, whatever is gracious,
if there is any excellence, if there is anything worthy of praise,
think about these things." It has been said that the vergers of
great cathedrals acquire a nobleness of bearing just by living under the lofty arches and in the light of the beautiful
stained glass. Perhaps that is true. Similarly we acquire a high-
mindedness by thinking on things that are lofty and good and
true. We develop a divine good taste which makes falsehood
and demagoguery and pretentiousness seem bad taste. And
remember, a person is never truly and safely good until his
taste is converted.

If we think this matter of taste is trivial, let us pause
a moment to see how even our hope of heaven depends on it.
Jesus said to his followers: "When I go and prepare a place
for you, I will come again and will take you to myself, that
where I am you may be also." But suppose that we have not
learned to like what Jesus liked. Then the place he has pre-

pared will not be heaven to us. If the only music a person likes is jazz, how will he enjoy a sonata?

If this girding ourselves with truth requires schooling, it also requires humility. The wise man is always modest enough to admit that he does not know it all. Sir Isaac Newton after all his scientific achievements likened himself to a boy playing with the pebbles on the shore of a vast ocean of knowledge.

Sometimes people ask whether Jesus will not some day be superseded by a greater teacher. My answer is No! And why? Because Christ so embodied the spirit of truth that he is as eternal as truth. He told his followers to pursue truth, asking, seeking, knocking. He taught them until the end of his earthly days. Then he said: "I have yet many things to say to you, but you cannot bear them now." Then he went on to promise them that the Holy Spirit, whom he termed the Spirit of truth, would continue with them to guide them into all truth. Christ opened a door to truth which never shuts and pointed a road to truth which never ends.

Furthermore in this schooling of ourselves in truth our own initiative is required if we are to put on the girdle of truth. Parents may guide a child by their points of view, but he must keep studying until he sees for himself. As the saying is, you can lead a boy to college, but you can't make him think. The church can pass on to us its creeds, but they do not become vital truth for us until we live our way into them.

Recall how Jesus once asked his disciples, "Who do men say that the Son of man is?" They spoke up and gave him the current opinions. They told their Master that some said he was Elijah come back to earth, some said he was John the Baptist, and some claimed that he was one of the prophets. But that did not satisfy Jesus. He put a more pointed question, asking, "But who do *you* say that I am?" Then

Simon Peter came forth with his great confession, "You are the Christ, the Son of the living God." Jesus answered, "Blessed are you, Simon Bar-Jona!" Why blessed? "For flesh and blood has not revealed this to you, but my Father who is in heaven. And I tell you, you are Peter, and on this rock I will build my church." That is, Simon was not just repeating what some other flesh-and-blood person had told him. He had reached his conviction that Christ is divine through his own firsthand experience. Therefore, he had become Peter, that is, "the rock." We of the Protestant faith believe that the church is founded not on Peter the man but on Peter's firsthand conviction of the deity of Christ. And remember, it was firsthand, gained through his own experience. When a person is gripped by a great experienced conviction, he has his loins girded with truth.

Yes, and it should be added that such gripping convictions come not by speculation but by action. We do not put on the girdle of truth merely by reason and argument. It is not enough to hear the truth and speak the truth. We must *do* the truth. That is why the Gospel closes the Sermon on the Mount with Jesus' warning that if any man hear his words and do them not, he shall be like a man who built his house on the sand, and the rains and wind came and beat upon that house, and it fell. But our Lord also promised that if any person heard his words and did them, he would be like a man who built his house on the rock, and though the storms came, it would stand.

By doing the truth when we hear it, we put a rock foundation under our faith. Yes, and thus we gird our loins with truth.

When we do school ourselves into truthfulness by thought and word and deed, our third question is, *"What does the girdle of truth do for us?"* One night I was riding home from a city in New England. At one end of my car the seats were arranged lengthwise of the train facing each other. Such an arrangement invites conversation. Two men came aboard who did not need any invitation to talk. They were fairly bursting to talk. They had apparently been imbibing from the cup that is supposed to cheer. But in their case it had not made them cheerful, but contentious. They began to talk about shoes, one asserting that you could always tell the quality of a man by his shoes. Well, that sounded as if they were getting at the bottom of things! So I listened further. In fact I could not help listening, for each one was saying, "I'll tell the world!" and their voices grew loud enough for much of the world to hear. As their conversation rattled on so inconsequentially and annoyingly, I thought how well they illustrated the lack of the girdle of truth. Their mental equipment was flapping about them in disorderly array. They were trying to fight for their opinions, but their armor hung loose. Their mental energies were scattered and unco-ordinated. Their words and thoughts were a mess of inconsistencies and incoherencies.

Now to a less degree of course, but nevertheless to some degree, all of us become loose and disjointed unless we have our loins girt with truth. But when one is belted with truth, it gives him a compactness and firmness. He is "all there" mentally with a coherence that gives a clear use of his faculties.

And truth also gives consistency as well as compactness. Few liars are clever enough to be consistent. Watch a witness who is trying to evade the truth in a court of law. He may be ever so shrewd and smooth. He may slip through knot after knot in which the cross-examining lawyer seeks to tie him. But give him enough rope and time, and he is almost sure to tie himself up in a tangle of inconsistency. Truth is too strong a force for men to tamper with without getting hurt. But if one has his eye single to truth, there is a straightforwardness about him which even his enemies will come to recognize and respect.

Moreover, to be girded with truth gives courage. If we have no weaknesses we are trying to conceal, if we are hiding behind no false fronts, if our gaze is not distracted by furtive glances to see if someone may find us out, then we gain courage. John Foster Dulles made a strong point in a Berlin conference when he said that we of the Western nations wanted "freedom from fear," whereas the Soviet leaders were motivated by the "fear of freedom." It behooves us to demonstrate in our civic and spiritual life that we are not afraid of real freedom.

The man girded with truth has also the strength of assurance. Feeling himself on the side of truth and knowing that truth is on the side of God, he has no fear of the final outcome. Such was the strength revealed in a very remarkable letter written by Captain Scott just before his death after reaching the South Pole. With Scott's party was a physician, Edward Wilson. Just before the end came, Scott penned a letter to Wilson's wife. In it he said:

If this letter reaches you, Bill [i.e., Dr. Wilson] and I will have gone out together. We are very near it now. . . . His eyes have a comfortable blue look of hope and his mind is peaceful with the satisfaction of his faith in regarding himself as part of the great scheme of the Almighty. I can do no more to comfort you than to tell you that he died as he lived, a brave, true man.

Yes, when one has studied and lived the truth to the best of his ability, he comes to trust God's care and keeping in life and death.

High above all human illustrations of this is the example of our Lord before Pilate. Note the contrast between Pilate and his prisoner. Pilate would listen to what the accusing priests had to say. Then he would rush out to hear what the crowd was calling. Then he would come in to Christ and ask him what he thought. Rushing around, Pilate grew more bewildered. He was guided only by expediency and the fear of having some of his past mistakes uncovered. His loins were not girded with truth, and his armor was hanging loose. In contrast there stood the Christ, calm, collected, unafraid. Why? Note his words to Pilate: "For this I was born, . . . to bear witness to the truth." The Christ stood with kingly dignity because his loins were girded with truth.

PRAYER:

Our Father, who hast put into our hearts such deep desires that we are restless without thee, forgive us for failing to see the truth and open our minds to the counsels of eternal wisdom. Grant us the honesty which hides behind no pretense and the courage to follow the facts, cost what it may. Make us sensitive to the sorrows of others and eager to share the burdens of the weak and the oppressed. Give us the grace to forgive those who despitefully use us and the humility to ask forgiveness of those we have wronged. Since we know not what the morrow may bring forth, arm us for the campaign of life with sound faith, sturdy hope, and persevering love. May we never grow weary in well-doing but help us to renew our strength through thy Spirit and be ever found faithful in the service of thy kingdom. We ask through Jesus Christ our Lord. Amen.

CHAPTER III

The Breastplate of Righteousness

OF WHAT DO WE THINK IN THE LORD'S PRAYER when we pray, "Deliver us from evil?" Do we think of the evils which may tempt us to wrongdoing or of the evil things which others may do to us? Do we think of the passions within ourselves which may become unruly or of the bad tempers of the world which threaten us with social tensions and global wars? Perhaps we have something of both in mind when we pray, "Deliver us from evil." Therefore, let us keep both in our thoughts as we consider the apostle Paul's counsel to put on "the whole armor of God."

The second piece of equipment which he mentions is "the breastplate of righteousness." The soldier of that period wore a breastplate or a coat of mail to protect the vital organs and especially the heart, which is the most vital of all. In spiritual warfare the heart is treated by the Bible as the seat of the emotions and the center of life's dynamic forces. The ancient proverb writer stressed its importance when he said, "Keep your heart with all vigilance; for from it flow the springs of life." Consider then how the breastplate of righteousness can protect our heart force.

First, it helps us to withstand *the evils which our enemies may inflict upon us*. To be sure, righteousness does not prevent enemies from attacking us. In fact, it may often invite attack. When a person of very superior goodness appears among us, it is not long before some people begin to say that he is "too good to be true." And these critics, instead

31

of trying to pull themselves up to a higher level, try to pull the nobler character down by ridicule or even by persecution.

Tolstoy in one of his books tells how lonely he was left in his search for virtue. When he tried to be truly good, he was met with contempt and ridicule. But when he gave way to his passions, he was encouraged and praised. History bears witness to the fact that the crowd tends to stone the prophets and pull the saints from their pedestals.

Jesus was charged by the Jerusalem crowd with being a disturber of the peace. It is hard for us to think of the gentle, loving Jesus as ever disturbing the peace. Certainly he was not an inciter of mobs and lawlessness. But if he had been just a purveyor of pleasing principles and soothing promises which make for peace of mind and social success, he would not have been crucified. He was far more than that. Jesus demonstrated a righteousness which so far exceeded the righteousness of the scribes and Pharisees that he disturbed their peace of mind. They were made uneasy and, no doubt, secretly ashamed by his perfection of character.

Moreover, Jesus stood for a spirit of freedom and a civic righteousness which disturbed the mental peace of the reactionary Sadducees, who were sitting rather pretty under the Roman government's regime. Yes, Jesus was looked upon by many in his day as a disturber of the peace. And he would be so regarded by many in our time if he were to return.

But while godly righteousness does not prevent others from attacking us, it does protect our hearts from being vitally wounded by their attacks. High thoughts can lift us above the reach of many a petty insult and irritating slight. High standards can hold us above the lure of many a low compromise and questionable expedience.

One time I flew out to San Francisco and back on a new DC-7. About a half hour after we left the West Coast, the captain's voice came back through the cabin saying something like this: "In about a minute the engines will slow down, but do not become alarmed. We are merely changing the supercharger. (At least that is what I think he said.) We are now at thirteen thousand feet, and we are going to increase the power so that we can climb to twenty thousand feet. It will take the engines a few seconds to make the shift." It was well that he told us in advance, for it is just a bit disconcerting to hear the engines slackening down when one is hanging thirteen thousand feet over Yosemite. But in a half minute the power zoomed on again, and we rose over the Sierras and the Rockies. The incident made me think of the prophet's words: "They who wait for the Lord shall renew their strength, they shall mount up with wings like eagles." When one feels himself empowered by righteousness, he rises above the range of many an evil which enemies can hurl against him.

And even if the arrows of attack do hit the godly man, they do not pierce to his heart and poison it. He does not become embittered, for the Lord helps him to understand how much misunderstanding is due to misinformation. Back in 1940 a paper was widely circulated with the aim of fighting the main interdenominational council of Protestantism. It listed the names of about twenty-five men who were leading in the large Federal Council. With the exception of myself they were men who commanded the respect and confidence of the church at large. But the circular labeled them all as "Termites in the Temple Gates." Now despite the attack I felt flattered to be included in the group. I did not mind being called a termite as long as I was in the company of such big bugs! Yet that document in varying forms has been kept in circulation, and I still receive some letters from people who think I am an enemy of the church. When I am tempted to become irritated by such attacks, I remember that the writers of the letters no doubt sincerely believe that I am dangerous, because of what they have read. That keeps me from getting bitter toward them, and also it makes me ask myself: May it not be that I am judging others as enemies toward me and toward what I believe simply because I am misinformed and do not understand them?

Some years ago a rival clergyman launched bitter attacks against the late George W. Truett, the beloved Baptist minister who for decades held such sway over the hearts of people in Dallas, Texas. Week after week this man would attack Truett in pulpit and press, but the saintly old gentleman never uttered a harsh word in reply. The result was that though the critic did not cease his attacks, the fires of controversy did not flare up but only served to warm the hearts of the people the more toward Truett. When love shows itself indestructible, it becomes irresistible.

Furthermore, the breastplate of righteousness can keep us from losing heart. During the dark days of the Dunkerque disaster, when it seemed that England was sure to be overrun by the Nazi hordes, Leslie Weatherhead, minister of London's City Temple, which was itself bombed to rubble, wrote these words:

God will win whether we win or lose. So in God, if we remain loyal to him, the victory will be ours, even if it looks like defeat and is called defeat and feels like defeat. The cross felt like defeat to Jesus and looked like defeat to the disciples and was called defeat by the world. Yet it was God's greatest victory. Let us then prepare for victory, be worthy of it and know how to apply it for God's purposes.

Yes, when a person really puts on a breastplate of righteousness, it protects his heart from being poisoned or defeated by the attacks of enemies.

Secondly, this breastplate protects us from *the evils which our friends and loved ones may do to us.*

Jesus said some words which seem hard to understand.

Note this: "A man's foes will be those of his own household."
Or take this statement, which seems harsher still: "Do you
think that I have come to give peace on earth? No, I tell you,
but rather division; for henceforth in one house there will be
five divided, three against two and two against three; they will
be divided, father against son and son against father, mother
against daughter and daughter against her mother."

How are we to understand such enigmatic statements?
Jesus stood for the stability of the home. He was against any
selfishness or infidelity which would weaken family ties. Yet
he also saw that sometimes love in its very desire to protect
may do damage to a soul by keeping it from its highest duty.
He himself faced the dangers which arise from love's desire
to protect. When he answered that he must go up to Jerusalem and suffer many things, even death, the devoted Peter
cried: "God forbid, Lord! This shall never happen to you."
Then Jesus turned and said to Peter: "Get behind me, Satan!
. . . You are not on the side of God, but of men."

And Jesus had to resist the protective desires of love
in his own family. Recall the occasion when he was teaching and word was brought to him that his mother and brothers
were outside looking for him. Why had they come? Undoubtedly it was to dissuade him from his exhausting and dangerous course. They saw it was leading him toward fatal conflict.
Thereupon Jesus cried: "Who are my mother and my
brothers?" And looking around, he said, "Here are my
mother and my brothers! Whoever does the will of God is my
brother, and sister, and mother."

As I understand them, those puzzling words were
spoken to show that family love, precious as it is, must not
restrain us from serving the whole family of God. Christ bids
us resist our dearest advisers when they would protect us from
our highest duty. He imparts the spirit of Wendell Phillips'
wife, who was an invalid. Each evening when the bold and

35

rugged reformer came to her bedside before going out to make his antislavery speeches before hostile audiences, she would take him by the hand and say, "Don't shilly-shally, Wendell."

When love would soften us by its protectiveness or narrow us by its possessiveness, then, as Jesus said, "a man's foes will be those of his own household." And then we need to put on the breastplate of righteousness.

We often hear it said that if people would just practice the Golden Rule, we would have a perfect society. If we would do unto others as we would that they should do unto us, all our tensions and strife would be over. A woman once said that to me, and I thought I had a very apt answer. "Yes," I replied, "the Golden Rule would be all we need provided we had sufficient imagination to know what we would want done to us if we were in the other person's place." But Henry Hitt Crane of Detroit has pointed out how much damage can be done by the Golden Rule if we were to rely solely on our own imaginations.

Suppose, for instance, your ten-year-old son comes to you and asks for something he desperately wants but is too young to handle without danger. Put yourself in the child's place. If you were a child and were to ask your father for a motorcycle or a gun or all the candy you could eat, would you want to be refused? Certainly not. Therefore, if you are to follow the Golden Rule of doing unto others as you would want done unto you, why not give the boy what he wants? Or, says Crane, suppose you are a judge on the bench and a prisoner is brought before you. Would you, if you were in the prisoner's place, want to be sentenced to the penitentiary? Of course not. Then why not follow the Golden Rule and free the poor fellow?

Ah, such considerations show us that the Golden Rule must be safeguarded by the measuring rod of righteousness. Our own eyes and imaginations are not enough to judge what we would want done to us if we were in the other person's place. We need the eye of God to give us the long view and to show us what is just and right in any given situation. And we need the breastplate of righteousness to safeguard us from the evils which even our loving purposes and good intentions might inflict upon us.

And now, in the third place, we need this breastplate to protect us against *the evils we may do to ourselves*.

Some time ago I heard it said of a man, "He is his own worst enemy." He is a very likable person. He is not being attacked by enemies. His foes are not in his own household or in his circles of friendships. But he is dissipating himself through drink. His fine mind is losing its firm grip. He is no longer quite dependable in his professional duties. He is sapping his own energies.

This matter of being one's own worst enemy is broader than any single besetting sin. One of my honored laymen, the late Edmund G. Vaughan, once called my attention to an intriguing title in Kipling's *Second Jungle Book*. The caption of the story was "Letting in the Jungle." In it Kipling gave a picture of the jungle surrounding a village in India. The beasts in the jungle plotted the downfall of the little human settlement. A migration of the elephants, lions, wild boars, and their bestial brothers moved toward the village. The crops were destroyed, the buildings peeled to pieces, the inhabitants driven away, and the settlement was left like an abandoned anthill. In the days of Kipling the jungle lay close upon the settlements of men in India.

In the United States and Canada the physical jungles have been pretty well cleared. But the moral jungle still lies close to our so-called civilization. When war comes, we see the bestial instincts turned loose. Frequent revelations of graft and vice and crime show how thin is the veneer of our culture. We desperately need the breastplate of righteousness to

37

protect us from the devastation wrought by our own unruly passions.

The heart is the seat of our emotions. It is capable of holy passions which provide the power for great living. But our great and noble passions can be dissipated in wasteful ways and distorted into destructive forces.

Consider anger, for instance. Anger is a God-given passion and wholesome when God-controlled. In the same letter to the Ephesians which describes the armor of God, Paul writes, "Be angry but do not sin." There is a sinless anger. The man who cannot be roused to righteous indignation by injustice and oppression, by cruelty to little children and helpless old age—that person is something less than a man.

But so many of us get angry about such little things. How often we hear a person say about something, "That just burns me up"! We let ourselves be consumed by little smoldering angers which never start any steam of reform. My friend, the late Paul Quillian, tells of a heart specialist who warned a man who was subject to these fits of anger. Said the doctor: "If you want to live longer, you must remember that when you tell a man where to get off, you get off there too." We need the breastplate of righteousness to protect us from the poisoned shafts of our own petty angers.

Or consider fear. Fear is a God-given passion. To say that we can and should get rid of all fear is Pollyanna poppycock. Jesus said: "Do not fear those who kill the body, and after that have no more that they can do. But I will warn you whom to fear; fear him who, after he has killed, has power to cast into hell." There is a just and holy fear. But how we waste our heart power by futile and foolish fears, by little anxieties and needless worries!

For several Sundays in the summer of 1941 just before Pearl Harbor I occupied the pulpit of the Central Union

Church in Honolulu. Over the chancel of that great church is inscribed a text of which I often think in these days of tension between East and West. There beyond Diamond Head pointing toward the Orient are these words: "Love Never Faileth."

Have we Christians of the West faith enough to believe the scripture we preach?

PRAYER:

Our Father, whose ways are higher than our ways as the heavens are high above the earth, we thank thee that despite all our misdeeds thou dost not disown us. May we feel sure of thy love, however hard our lot, and confident of thy help, however heavy our burden. More and more fill us with that sympathy for other's troubles which comes from forgetfulness of our own. Grant that we may be earnest in work, fair in play, and faithful even in that which is least. Keep alive in us the spirit of adventure, that we may greet our tomorrows with eager expectancy. Cleanse us from all false pride, intolerance, and contempt, that with humility of spirit we may enter into fellowship with those who are working for peace and brotherhood. Guide, guard, and govern us even to the end. We ask through Jesus Christ our Lord. Amen.

CHAPTER IV

The Sandals of Peace

THE CRY FOR PEACE IS AS OLD AS THE DAWN OF history and as fresh as the morning newspaper. Several centuries before Christ the prophet Isaiah broke forth into lyric longing, saying, "How beautiful upon the mountains are the feet of him who brings good tidings, who publishes peace." And when the Hebrew seers foretold the coming of a divine Deliverer, they said his name would be "Wonderful Counselor, Mighty God, Everlasting Father, Prince of Peace." Then in the fullness of time when the Saviour was born, the note struck by the angelic chorus in the nativity story of the shepherds was, "On earth peace among men with whom [God] is pleased." The Bible taken in its full sweep is a gospel of peace.

It is not surprising, therefore, that when the apostle Paul comes to describe the armor of God which the Christian is to put on, he should include the element of peace. This third item in the armor he lists thus: *"And having shod your feet with the equipment of the gospel of peace."*

But when we hear a soldier being told that his mission is peace, there are many in our generation who greet such an announcement with mirthless, cynical laughter. They have heard it too often to believe it. In World War I our soldiers were summoned to fight with the assurance that it was a war to end war. When less than twenty-five years later our sons and daughters were called to the colors again, we did not have the heart to promise them that it was a war to insure peace. We simply told them it was a war of survival.

Now in our atomic age if a third global conflict involves us, we can hardly call it a war of survival. Our most trusted seers tell us that civilization cannot survive an all-out world conflict with atomic weapons. Wars have become so fearful and so futile that they leave nothing to promise the fighters.

Hence when Paul bids the Christian soldier put on the armor of God and fight for peace, we are skeptical. What new and convincing thing can be said on this old theme? Let us consider what the Apostle would include in what he calls "the equipment of the gospel of peace."

First, I think Paul would put *an orderly inner personal life*. The Chinese have a proverb that the longest journey begins with the first step. The Christian peacemaker must start with God and himself. It is worth noting that Paul puts the breastplate of righteousness just ahead of the sandals of peace. Righteousness is the preparation for peace. Remember, too, that Jesus in listing the Beatitudes puts "Blessed are the pure in heart" just before "Blessed are the peacemakers." He who would make peace must first bring his own life into harmony with God.

The Epistle of James asks, "What causes wars, and what causes fightings among you? Is it not your passions that are at war in your members?" Of course it would be an oversimplification of our world situation to imply that the warring passions within ourselves cause the present tensions between nations, for there are ideological and dynastic issues involved.

Nevertheless, just as we can study the elements of the ocean in a drop of sea spray, so we can see the germs of war making by observing the passions within ourselves. Consider pride, for instance, the first of the so-called seven deadly sins. Pride makes the individual touchy, ever desirous of saving

41

face. If he is not successful, pride gives him an inferiority complex. And if he is successful, he never finds enough room even at the top. Now consider how much the factor of face-saving enters into the attitudes of oriental races and nations which have been hitherto kept down by colonial powers. Also consider how pride has gone to the head of powerful nations like Russia, aye, how pride has affected the outlook of white peoples the world over. Yes, in our own inner lives we can see the elements which compose the ocean of world restlessness.

Moreover, the unsettled conflicts of the inner life feed into the currents of world strife. The person whose own passions are out of control makes for restlessness around him. The man who is frustrated or feels inferior is ready material for the demagogue and the agitator. The person who feels handicapped by poverty or injustice is an easy prey to Communism or Fascism.

Now the Christian gospel of peace is that inner orderliness, and peace can come only through righteousness. We may think at times that we can relieve our inner tensions by yielding to our lower desires. The prodigal son may have felt for a time free and easy in the far country of unrestrained indulgence. But when he came to himself, he yearned for a higher life. Likewise, Francis Thompson, the London medical student, ran the gamut of worldly pleasure. But the thrills did not last. Ever pursuing him was what he called the "Hound of Heaven," the voice of the Christ, saying, "All things betray thee, who betrayest Me." We human beings are so made that we cannot be free whole selves on the lower level of animal desire.

Paul saw this when he cried, "I pommel my body and subdue it." And he explained, "I see in my members another law at war with the law of my mind and making me captive to the law of sin." Then he said, "Thanks be to God through

42

Jesus Christ our Lord!" He yielded his inner life to Christ's control. His first "equipment of the gospel of peace" is an orderly inner life.

And having brought his personal life into God's control, the soldier of Christ in the second place equips himself with *a creative good will*. In 1933 King George V of England made a Christmas broadcast which attracted wide attention because of both its content and the character of the monarch who made it. Frail, fatherly King George said to his people as they faced the dark days of the 1930's: "Unshakable sanity, invincible patience and tireless good will are the foundations for seeing us through the difficulties ahead."

Peacemaking calls for tireless and creative good will. Paul said that "God was in Christ reconciling the world to himself" and that Christ had committed to us the ministry of reconciliation. The Christian is called to be a reconciler. Or to put it in modern business terms, he is called to be a trouble shooter.

God's trouble shooter radiates good will even by his thoughts. Having pure motives in his own mind, he imputes worthy motives to others, giving the benefit of the doubt wherever possible. When trouble is brewing in any group, we usually know the persons who can give us the "low-down." Even a minister knows members of his church from whom he can get the "low-down" when there is ferment in his parish, for they have their ears to the ground to catch the rumors. But we also know persons who live on a higher level and lift others up.

The peacemaker also radiates good will by his words. He speaks his convictions when a moral issue is at stake, but he speaks the truth in love. He is not one of those who, like many a press columnist and news commentator, likes to play on people's passions and hatreds. It is easier to arouse people *against* something than *for* something. The reason for that

43

is understandable. It is the same psychology which will bring thousands of people to see a fellow knocked out in a prize fight while only a few medical students go around to the hospital the next day to see him put together again. People like to see a fight, and the speaker or writer who can arouse a fighting mood against someone is popular. But the Christian does not seek such popularity. He tries to stir sympathy and good will.

Furthermore, the Christian peacemaker is a reconciling force by his deeds as well as by his thoughts and words. He does not merely discuss racial and religious differences as problems; but he enters into experiences of fellowship with individuals of other groups. He prepares for world citizenship by practicing the principles of brotherhood in his own community, for he knows that if we cannot get along with our neighbors, it is futile to talk about a family of nations. If we cannot keep our word as man to man, we cannot expect treaties to be kept between nation and nation.

If this is a government of the people and for the people and by the people, we the people must so think and talk and act that the contagion of our peacemindedness will counteract the warmindedness which has gripped so many peoples and governments of the world. Peacemaking is your business and mine, and we cannot delegate it to the professional soldiers and diplomats.

Also we must keep in mind Paul's principle of overcoming evil with good. When we try to counteract evildoers by adopting their methods, we are being defeated by them. I sometimes fear that we in the United States are in danger of copying certain Soviet methods in trying to counteract Communism. Evil is to be driven out as darkness is to be driven out. And how do we drive out darkness? We cannot drive it out with our fists or a sword. We must turn on the light. So in fighting evils, whether they be Communism or corruption

44

or hysteria, the effective way is to turn on goodness and reason.

I believe there are still some good things which we Amercians can do through our government and through the churches to soften the hearts of people and nations now suspicious of us. When I saw some of the agricultural and engineering projects aided by our government in India, and when I saw the work of our devoted missionaries in India and Pakistan, I was confirmed in my belief that there are ways of reconciliation still open which might reach even through some so-called curtains. When we persevere in good will, we touch the hand of Him who "is able to do far more abundantly than all that we ask or think."

And along with an orderly inner life and a creative good will there is a third element in the equipment of the gospel of peace. This is *an organized fellowship.*

The man who puts on the armor of God is not meant to fight alone. He is to serve in the army of the Lord. This letter to the Ephesians which describes the armor of God also depicts the sweeping fellowship of the church and the whole family of God.

There is something in human nature which thrills to a fight and something which also craves fellowship. We have a common saying that men like a fighter and also a saying that all the world loves a lover. Christ was a fighter. He said: "Do not think that I have come to bring peace on earth; I have not come to bring peace, but a sword." As I understand those words, he was calling his followers to be as brave and inventive and devoted in his service as the soldier is in war. But Christ calls men to fight for fellowship, not against it.

Herein lies one major difference between Christ's attitude and our own. Christ fought the evil but loved the evil-doers. We fight the evildoers and then keep the evil. We kill the warriors but preserve the war system.

Can we wage peace without hatred and slaughter?

45

Can we take over into the peace movement some of the great rallying concepts which have hitherto been monopolized by the war makers?

Consider patriotism, for example. When we think of a patriotic society, we think of one which commemorates military achievements. When we stage a patriotic celebration, we do it with military accouterments, tanks, guns, and the like. But can we stir patriotic sentiments by peaceful methods as well as by warlike ones? Why not? Why can we not effect the same transformation in our love of country as in our love of persons? There was a time when men thought that they had to arouse a woman's love by fighting for it with physical prowess. The medieval knight won his fair lady in tournaments of force. But today if it were known that two suitors had waged a fight over a woman's hand, it is fairly certain that neither would get her. Men do not fight for ladies' hands, except in a night-club brawl.

There was a time when public leaders won their following by physical prowess, as in the day of Saul, who was chosen first king of Israel because of his stature and strength. But if a leader in our government should stoop to settle his quarrels by physical combat, he would lose the public's respect. Bitter as some of our current political bickerings are, they have not been lowered to the level of fist fights.

If we have wrought such a change in our appraisal of persons, we can do likewise in our attitude toward governments. We can educate ourselves to feel the thrill of pride and love when our country is showing her helpfulness with gifts and service rather than when she is demonstrating her destructiveness with bombs. If our homes and schools and churches set themselves to it, they can make patriotism as colorful and challenging in peace as in war.

Also we can take over into the peace movement the concept of propaganda which, like patriotism, has hitherto been almost monopolized by war. A newspaper some time ago admitted that propaganda required hostile emotions to spur it. But must it ever be so?

I asked a distinguished educator if he could see any hope of changing the hostile propaganda of nations. He suggested that I make a fresh study of St. Francis of Assisi. St. Francis lived in the time of the medieval Crusades. Peter the Hermit and other Crusaders aroused Europe to a frenzy of hatred against the Moslems who held the Holy Land. They strewed the bodies of the Crusaders over the Near East in their efforts to rescue the Holy Sepulcher. St. Francis, on the other hand, went around preaching love and radiating a reconciling spirit. The glow of his goodness lives on.

Are we not seeing a situation somewhat like that of the old crusaders? The West is being aroused against the East, the East against the West. If the tension keeps growing, the clash will come. Is it too late to reawaken the spirit of St. Francis of Assisi, the spirit of love which tries to embrace the whole family of God? Certainly the church of Christ can attempt nothing less.

And who can measure the power of the church? In 1933 Hitler boasted to an associate: "I promise you that if I wished to, I could destroy the church in a few years. It is hollow and false and rotten through and through. One push and the whole structure would collapse. . . . Its day has gone."

Had a spokesman of the German church been present he might have answered as Théodore Beza did to a similar boast by the king of Navarre in the sixteenth century: "Sire, it is the lot of the church in whose name I speak to receive blows, not to inflict them. But may it please your Majesty to remember that the church is an anvil which has worn out many hammers." Yes, and we might say that, though the road of the peacemaker is rough, the Christian's sandals of peace are sturdy enough for the journey.

PRAYER:

Our Father in heaven, look down, we beseech thee, on thy troubled children. Give light, to those who sit in darkness and love to those who live in coldness. Grant us the faith to keep going when the road is hard and to remain good when the way is easy. Help us to be loyal to the best we know until we learn more fully what is best. Restrain the angry passions of men until reason may be heard. Illumine our insights with love and fill our hearts with hope that we may show our best to others and bring out the best in others. May we find such peace within our own minds that we may be a refuge and strength to our friends. Guide the president of the United States and all other leaders of the world that they may seek peace and pursue it until men shall learn war no more. We ask through Jesus Christ our Lord. Amen.

CHAPTER V

The Shield of Faith

THERE WAS A TIME WHEN THE HOUSE OF GOD offered physical safety. In England four hundred years ago persons pursued by their enemies could fling themselves across the threshold of a cathedral, crying "sanctuary," and they were safe from attack. Even those who were fleeing from the law, except in crimes of treason or sacrilege, could rush into church and be exempt from arrest, regardless of guilt or innocence.

But no longer does the church afford such protection. The House of God is no shelter from the arm of the law or the attack of invaders. Nor was the Christian church a place of physical safety in its earliest days. Quite the opposite. To join the Christian church was to enter the danger zone in the time of the Caesars.

Hence when the apostle Paul bade his Christian converts to put on the armor of God, he was not offering it as a protection against bodily dangers. It had not preserved him from physical perils. Note his own experience. He wrote:

Five times I have received . . . the forty lashes less one. Three times I have been beaten with rods; once I was stoned. Three times I have been shipwrecked; a night and a day I have been adrift at sea; . . . in danger from rivers, danger from robbers, danger from my own people, danger from Gentiles.

If bodily protection were the purpose of God's armor, then Paul was a poor demonstrator of its value. But the

49

apostle was primarily concerned about arming the mind and spirit so that what happened to the body would not hurt or embitter or destroy the soul. To that end he offered the girdle of truth, the breastplate of righteousness, the sandals of peace. And now as the fourth equipment in the armor of God he says: *"above all taking the shield of faith, with which you can quench all the flaming darts of the evil one."*

How does the shield of faith help to protect us from the world's evils? First, by a protecting *calm*. Paul says, "The peace of God, which passeth all understanding, shall keep your hearts and minds through Christ Jesus." We talk much about peace of mind. Multitudes are seeking inner peace by adjustment to outer circumstances. They think they will find peace if their business is made to go well, if friends flock around, and the body is relaxed and comfortable. But how can one have peace under physical hardships such as Paul endured?

For one thing faith in God calms us with a sense of his continuing presence when the things we care for are taken away. When a tragic sorrow befell my family circle and cut short a beloved life, we went down for a few days to the beautiful old city of Charleston, South Carolina. There on the one side we beheld the ocean, whose waves beat restlessly against the shore but were ever replenished from the bosom of the enduring sea. The ocean suggests the changeless amid the changing. On the other side of the city were the lovely magnolia gardens, vivid reminders of the renewing life which ever breaks through the blight of winter to bring blossom and beauty. The sea and the gardens served to recall Elizabeth Barrett Browning's mood when she wrote:

I smiled to think God's greatness flowed around our incompleteness,—
Round our restlessness, His rest.

50

Also faith in God protects us with a calming sense of steadying strength. In 1940 I was in Mexico City on election day. From my hotel room I could look down into Constitution Square. All day the shouting partisans surged back and forth in groups. At about four o'clock in the afternoon some bullets began to fly. But above the mob in the distance I could see the snow-clad peaks of the two great extinct volcanoes Popocatepetl and Iztaccihuatl. Their majestic summits rising above the shouting, turbulent crowds reminded me of the Psalmist's words: "I lift up my eyes to the hills . . . Whence does my help come? My help comes from the Lord, who made heaven and earth." The mountains stood silent and strong in contrast to the noisy, restless people; and I felt like saying with Emerson, "Why so hot, little man?"

And this silent, peaceful, calming strength which is seen in nature is also to be seen in human nature. When John Wesley was returning to England from his missionary experience in Georgia, his ship was engulfed in a heavy storm at sea. He was frightened. But there were two Moravian missionaries on board who seemed utterly unafraid. Wesley saw that they had a faith and poise which he did not possess. He sought their secret. His search led him eventually to the deep heart-warming experience from which the Methodist movement stemmed.

What is the secret of that inner calm which can withstand the attacks of evil and trouble? Hear the testimony of Cardinal Mercier, who along with King Albert I of Belgium so heroically rallied the besieged Belgians during World War I. Mercier said:

Whether in the years of peace or the years of war, whether in poverty or prosperity, whether in failure or success, never have I failed to feel deep down in my heart a sense of tranquility, confidence and peace. . . . I must tell you the secret of Christian

51

serenity. It lies in giving yourself confidently to the goodness of the Lord.

Now we are getting close to the meaning of what the apostle Paul called "the peace of God, which passeth all understanding." Recall how he discovered it. He was born Saul of Tarsus. He was by nature a man of strong emotions and sharp tensions. He set out to crush the rising new Christian sect which he felt was undermining the faith of his fathers. He went around "breathing out threatenings and slaughter," as he said. He held the garments of the men while they stoned Stephen for preaching this new Christian heresy. As the stones fell on Stephen's breaking body, the martyr looked up with steadfast face and cried, "I see the heavens opened, and the Son of man standing at the right hand of God." Not only did Stephen keep his poise, but he also prayed, "Lord, do not hold this sin against them."

Saul saw that Stephen had something which he lacked. What power could sustain a man's faith and forgiving spirit when he was being stoned to death? The query haunted Saul and would not let him rest. Then on the road to Damascus the light broke on his mind, and the resistance of his resentful heart gave way. In the days of meditation and seclusion which followed, Saul surrendered his spirit and consecrated his will to the Christ whom he had formerly hated. He became Paul the apostle. He so entered into fellowship with Christ that his personal interests merged with his Lord's and lifted him above the worries and evils which formerly had bedeviled him. Thenceforth his faith was as a shield with which he quenched the "flaming darts of the evil one."

Secondly, faith in God is a shield which provides a protecting *conscience*. When Paul was on trial before the Roman governor at Caesarea, he said: "I always take pains," or as the King James Version puts it, "I exercise myself."

The Creator puts a conscience into the original equipment of each person. But he does not guarantee to keep it in condition. Our consciences, like our bodies, need care and exercise to keep them fit. The conscience must be watched even more closely than the body, because its illnesses do not always make themselves known by aches and pains. A sluggish liver gives one a dyspeptic feeling of discomfort, but a sluggish conscience may give us a feeling of exhilaration. It may make one feel that he is having the time of his life, with no inhibitions to give him pause.

It takes pains to keep a conscience truly clear. Sometimes a person thinks his conscience is clear simply because his head is empty. He has not informed himself sufficiently to see the issues involved.

And it takes pains to keep one's conscience free. We Americans believe in the separation of church and state. We want no church dictating to the state and no government muzzling the pulpit. But consciences may be free from enslavement to church and state and yet not be truly free. Some consciences are free as a stray dog is free. A stray dog, having no master, will likely follow any passer-by who whistles to it. Similarly many persons fall in behind any passing prejudice or whistling crowd. Such are the persons of whom mobs are made. Such are the pliable weaklings who play into the hands of demagogues and dictators and rabble-rousers. Paul believed that a conscience becomes truly free only when it is following the highest Master it can know. Then it is free because it is fulfilling the function for which it is given.

And when we do take pains to develop a good conscience, free and clear, it proves itself a shield to ward off the attacks of temptations before they reach the mind and heart. Some years ago Harold Begbie drew a contrast between Mrs. Gladstone and Lady Asquith, both of them wives of former British premiers. I do not vouch for the accuracy of his appraisal. I only give you his estimate. Begbie said that Mrs. Asquith, though a woman of probity and virtue, had such a mercurial temperament and inquisitive spirit that she liked to entertain tempting thoughts in the vestibule of her mind; whereas Mrs. Gladstone had such a finely trained conscience and such firm convictions that temptations which intrigued Mrs. Asquith never got inside the door of her thinking. Whether that distinction applied to the two women mentioned, I do not know. But it is true that some consciences are so easy of entrance that temptations do get in, and, like the slick house-to-house salesman, if they get one foot in the door, the morning is spoiled. A good conscience is a shield that wards off many temptations before they get into our thoughts.

There is a curious difference between our estimates of the trouble we can stand and our estimates of the temptations we can withstand. We look ahead at some possible calamity, and we say, "I don't believe I could ever stand that." But if such a disaster does overtake us, we do stand it. On the other hand, we look ahead at some possible temptation, and we say, "Oh, I could resist that." But alas, too often if it comes, we do not withstand it. It is strange but true that trouble or suffering often brings out the strength we did not know we had, while temptation reveals the weakness we did not know we had. We need to develop in advance a conscience so disciplined that, when temptation flies at us, we shall have a shield of faith to ward it off.

And we need to be prepared not only against sudden and unexpected temptations but also against yielding to those evils which wear down our resistance by constant contact.

> Vice is a monster of so frightful mien,
> As to be hated needs but to be seen;

Yet seen too oft, familiar with her face,
We first endure, then pity, then embrace.[1]

At the portal of my church were placed four marble pillars when the building was erected. But the delicate texture of that Italian marble cannot withstand our New York weather. Two of those pillars have had to be replaced, and the other two are preserved only by repeated treatment. Some human characters there are that disintegrate in our metropolitan moral weather. Exposed to the foggy compromises, the frosty cynicism, the stormy temptations, they go to pieces. They need repeated coatings of Christian faith to shield them from the destructive elements.

When the famous trial of eleven Communists was on in 1949, Judge Harold Medina, who presided, was subjected to all sorts of tricks and irritations to wear him down and cause him to lose his temper or do something which would give occasion for a retrial. How did he keep his poise? Note his testimony: "I sought strength from the one Source that never fails."

And now along with a protecting calm and a protecting conscience, the shield of faith gives a protecting *courage*. If we are normal human beings, we begin life with a certain endowment of courage. It may vary in amount somewhat according to temperament, but each of us has some. The apostle Paul recognized this when he said to young Timothy, "Rekindle the gift of God that is within you . . . ; for God did not give us a spirit of timidity but a spirit of power and love and self-control."

Each of us can do something to stir up our native courage. We can use our bodies to help us. Boys sometimes whistle in the dark to keep up their courage. I was never very

[1] Alexander Pope, *Essay on Man.*

good at whistling. As a boy on an Ohio farm I had the duty of helping with the chores. If we happened to get home late, I had to bring the cows in from the back pasture after dark. With my imagination I could see moving shadows in the woods and hear strange noises if I stopped to listen. So I did not stop to listen. I walked as fast as I could and talked to the cows on the way. My first experience in public speaking was to cows, and I think they helped me almost more than any audience I have had since! Suffice it to say, talking to a cow or a dog or to oneself helps a boy to keep up his courage.

And as we grow more mature, we can do other things to stir up our native courage. We can do what Thomas Carlyle did. Once in Paris he went through a three weeks' period of almost total sleeplessness and despair. He entertained thoughts of self-destruction. But one day he asked himself what he was afraid of and what was the worst it could do to him. If worst came to worst, could he endure it? He finally decided that in no event would he go through life whimpering like a coward, but that whatever came, he would meet it and defy it. From that hour he dated his new birth of courage.

But Christ gives a better way of kindling courage than Carlyle found. Jesus did not manifest his courage because his back was to the wall but because his face was toward his heavenly Father. Christian courage is born not of desperation but of dependence on God.

Robert Christenberry, head of a big New York hotel, has told of his despondency on his way home from France after World War I. How could he live a full life with his right arm gone? The answer came out of his grandfather's Bible. Here it is: "If God is for us, who is against us?" Those are the words of the apostle Paul and reveal how his faith kept up his courage.

The Christian faith is a shield which gives a protecting courage also when sickness lays us low. A friend of mine, who is a very busy physician, was stricken and flat on his back when the summit of Mount Everest was reached. From his sickbed Harold Noyes penned these lines:

> Earth's high point feels the goal-won tread of man;
> No more allures the peak, earth's tallest rock
> Is conquered!
> By camp and camp man can
> Gain upwards. . . .
>
> A comrade gone! Push on, nor count the price
> A wild wind's shriek laments for martyrs lost;
> On treacherous crevasse snow-bridges sway;
> And now—the pinnacle, white plume tossed;
> In thinning breath, how slow steps creep the way!
> Is this the last adventure? Ends man's dream
> With Everest o'ertopped? No, Higher gleam
> Till the last heart-beat, the last throb of time.
> Dare man to vision triumphs. Risk a
> nobler climb![2]

With such Christian faith a person is shielded from being depressed or defeated by anything that comes. Like Paul we can say:

Who shall separate us from the love of Christ? Shall tribulation, or distress, or persecution, or famine, or nakedness, or peril, or sword? . . . No, in all these things we are more than conquerors through him who loved us. For I am sure that neither death, nor life, . . . nor things present, nor things to come, . . . nor anything else in all creation, will be able to separate us from the love of God in Christ Jesus our Lord.

PRAYER:

O God, thou source of the light that never fades and of the life that never ends, we give three humble and hearty

---

[2] Written in a personal letter to me and used by permission of the author.

thanks for thy wonderful works to the children of men. We thank thee for our dreams and the will to realize them, for interest in our work and power to do it, for the trusts committed to us and the desire to keep faith with those who believe in us. Make us worthy of the rich inheritances of our common life, the laws that protect us, the families that care for us, the churches which inspire us. Dispel our foolish fears and arouse us to our real dangers. Teach us how to live and work together that we may banish the shadows of strife and use the bounties of the good earth for the building of a better world. May the desire to help be so great that none shall have the desire to hurt. Set our hearts on things eternal that time may lose its terrors. We ask through Jesus Christ our Lord. Amen.

CHAPTER VI

The Helmet of Hope

IN OUR STUDY OF THE ARMOR OF GOD, WE NOW come to the helmet. Here at least is one piece of equipment still used in modern warfare. Breastplates and shields, sandals and swords, may be of little use in today's fighting. But helmets are still important. When missiles fall out of the skies, soldiers wear helmets. And now with the prospect of poison gas we see pictures of head coverings with hideous snouts and giant goggles.

But what kind of helmet does the Bible offer? Here is Paul's statement: "And take the helmet of salvation." And in his first letter to the Thessalonians, the fifth chapter, Paul is a bit more explicit. He says, "And for a helmet [take] the hope of salvation."

To offer hope as a helmet for our protection does not sound very convincing at first, does it? Hope so often deceives us into trusting false protection. Hope has been likened to the rattle which Mother Nature puts into the hands of man, her fretful child, to keep him quiet while he is cutting his teeth on the hard facts of reality. Hope keeps the gambler throwing away his money in expectation of a winning streak. Hope lures the criminal further into the coils of crime, foolishly counting on beating the racket. In fact, hope so often misleads that the modern tendency of writers is to think they must be pessimistic in order to be realistic.

Well, one can say at the outset that Paul was no "born optimist." In his youth he was quite the opposite. He had a tendency to look on the dark side of things. For instance, when he saw the rise of the new Christian sect, he did not say to his fellow Jews: "Don't worry; things will work out all right." He became so frantically worried that he set out to fight the new movement. In short, Paul was a converted pessimist. At least then we can be sure his helmet of hope was not made from wishful thinking.

First then, let us look at the elements which went into the making of Paul's hope. He saw hope as one of the raw materials of life which abide. "So faith, hope, love abide, these three." And they abide because they are an integral part of man's make-up.

Some years ago my eye was caught by the picture of a boy and his dog in a field watching a train recede into the distance. There was a light in the lad's face not reflected in the dog's eyes. The boy was obviously following the train in his fancy, probably dreaming of the day when he could go to faraway places in search of his fortune. His eyes were alight with hope.

The years pass. The boy grows to manhood and begins his work. It may be on the farm or in the factory or office. But the train keeps running, the train of thought carrying his hopes of positions he some day may fill.

A girl crosses his path. He falls in love. He plights his troth. He plans a home. His hopes now enlarge with love. Perhaps children are born to that home. His hopes lengthen to include their careers. He realizes that he will not reach all the goals of his dreams. But he sees his children carrying on beyond his reach.

Disappointments come to that home. Death may invade. Anxiety plays with his sick heart at times as a cat plays with a captive mouse, letting it run free for a little time, then pouncing on it again with cruelty. Yet through all the shadows he lives and loves and laughs and hopes. Hope abides.

The years pass. His eyes are dimmer, and his steps are slower. But his train of thought still carries his hopes. As far as his earthly life is measured, the train is running downgrade. It is coming into the terminal. But if he has faith, he discovers, as did the late John Buchan, governor-general of Canada, that when you are going down hill, the long vistas are in front of you; whereas when you are climbing a hill, you have to look around to get the long view. So as he descends the hill of the years, his vista lengthens and his hopes run on into that land which "no eye has seen."

Even if he lacks religious faith, he still hopes. Recall what Robert Ingersoll, the famous agnostic, said when he stood at the grave of his brother: "In the night of Death Hope sees a star and listening Love can hear the rustling of a wing."

Yes, from boyhood to life's last border our trains of thought continue to run and carry our cargoes of hope. But now are these hopes to be trusted, or are they only empty cartons of dreams? C. S. Lewis, the Oxford teacher who is so widely accepted as an interpreter of Christianity, tells us that for a period of his life he became an atheist. He could not accept the glib answers given to explain why God allows so much evil in the world. Therefore he gave up believing in God.

But then he began to realize the dilemma into which he was tossed by his denial of God's existence. If there is no intelligent Creator or plan back of this universe, how can we trust our own reasoning power? Our mental processes would then be due to accidental arrangements and rearrangements of the atoms in our brain, giving us the sensation of thought. If such were the case, then by nodding our heads we might shake up some new thoughts. But I have been preaching long enough to learn that, when people nod their heads, they are not always thinking new thoughts. Nodding heads may mean that the thinking process has stopped.

61

If we are to live, we must trust our own reasoning powers as being purposeful not accidental. If we cannot trust our own reason, then we are not justified in saying, "I do not believe in God," or in expressing any other belief. If we are to be guided at all by our own intelligence, we must believe in a Creator who makes human intelligence trustworthy. So C. S. Lewis reasoned, and thus he was brought back to belief in God.

Now the apostle Paul was in line with the Oxford professor's reasoning. And he also saw that if we are to trust our reasoning processes as usable, we are also justified in using our hopes. For hope is an essential part of thought. Take away all hope, and see how soon the mind runs off the track. Paul was, therefore, speaking as a good psychologist when he said we must cover our heads with the helmet of hope. Otherwise we lose our minds.

Hence if we need belief in God in order to trust our own reasoning power, we can claim him as one who justifies us in our processes of hope. And so Paul refers to God as "the God of hope."

Thus we see that Paul's helmet of hope is made out of material as integral to our lives as are our minds and bodies.

And now in the second place let us go on to observe *how Paul fashioned the raw materials of hope into a helmet of salvation.* He tells us the steps: "Tribulation worketh patience; and patience, experience; and experience, hope" (K.J.V.) I like Professor Edwin Aubrey's translation of those lines. He does it thus: "The pressures of life develop staying power, and staying power develops competence, and competence develops hope."

If we are to find assuring hope, we must develop patience, or staying power. This is not a very popular virtue with us, is it? Modern living tends to make us more impatient than in biblical times. In those days men made their living largely from the soil, and they had to be patient with the seasons. When they traveled by land, they had to adjust their gait to the beasts of burden. When they traveled by sea, they were pretty dependent on winds. But we live in a machine age. We drive motor cars which do not seem to tire. The multitudes who live in cities do not have to adjust themselves to the slow processes of the soil. But while we can raise January strawberries in hothouses, we must remember that we cannot raise the fruits of the spirit—love, joy, peace, and their like—by hothouse methods. While we can turn on the light in a room by pressing a button, we must remember that we cannot turn on the light of hope in a dark world by quick mechanical means. We must "wait on the Lord" if we are to renew our spirit and strength.

And remember, patience does not always mean slowing down. As Aubrey says, it means staying power. And staying power develops competence. Someone has defined a diamond as "a piece of coal which stayed on the job." There is only a fraction of truth in such a statement, for coal is plentiful and diamonds are very rare. Not everyone who stays put develops into a diamond. He may just "get stuck in the mud." Nevertheless, it is true that people often lose out because they lack staying power. They leave for greener pastures just before the grass starts growing on their own plot. They do not stick by until the winning blow is struck. "To hold on when there's nothing left save the will which says 'hold on'"—that is one mark of a man, as Kipling said, to hold on until we reach "the end of our string," as we say, and then still to hold on. It is then that we touch the one who "is able to do far more abundantly than all that we ask or think, according to the power that worketh in us."

Yonder is a boy in school who seems dull. He cannot keep up with the class. The others are beginning to think him hopeless. But a patient teacher takes a special interest in the lad. She perseveres until she finds one thing which he can do and do well. That one thing gives him a feeling of competence, and from that as a starting point he begins to go ahead. He gains hope in himself. An experience like this is often repeated in the schoolrooms of our country.

One of the most heartening things to me is the fact that those who stay by and work most perseveringly with our so-called social problems do gain confidence in their solution. Take the problem of youth, for instance. One time I delivered a series of five broadcasts to youth. In preparing those messages I read many books and articles on the conditions of our young people. But I think the most illuminating and convincing single document I read was a little brochure containing the rules and bylaws of a girls' club in New York in a section commonly called "Hell's Kitchen." This group of girls had drawn up an expression of social ideals and a set of rules for social conduct which were most inspiring. They strengthened immeasurably my hope in youth.

Or consider a section of New York City which is so much discussed as the most difficult area. Some time ago I talked with the principal of the high school in that region. He is a man who has worked among the people there for over thirty years. Is he hopeless about the solution of their social problems? Not at all! He can cite uncounted cases of youth who have come up to splendid careers in that section. It is worth noting that hope is developed in those who show staying power under adverse conditions, whereas pessimism is likely to be found among those in luxurious penthouses or retired positions who look down and discuss the so-called problems of youth and race and poverty.

It is not broad, glittering generalities which generate hope but contact with local situations.

One of the most formative American preachers in my boyhood days was Washington Gladden of Columbus, Ohio.

He was ever holding up the ideals of racial brotherhood and world peace. But he could not always see his way through. How did he recover hope? By observing and doing the duties near at hand. He said:

> I know that right is right;
> That it is not good to lie;
> That love is better than spite,
> And a neighbor than a spy;
>
> .   .   .   .
>
> In the darkest night of the year,
> When the stars are all gone out,
> That courage is better than fear,
> That faith is truer than doubt.

Then having started with these simple first principles and local applications, Gladden attained hope in the ultimate outcome. He said further:

> And fierce though the fiends may fight,
> And long though the angels hide,
> I know that Truth and Right
> Have the universe on their side;
>
> And that somewhere, beyond the stars,
> Is a Love that is better than fate;
> When the night unlocks her bars
> I shall see Him, and I will wait.

Gladden like Paul found that staying power or patience develops competence and competence develops hope.

Having seen how Paul found and fashioned the materials which made his hope, let us now observe *how hope is a helmet of salvation.*

For one thing, it saves the individual with the hope of life beyond this world. Paul's letters are filled with confidence about life after death. He cries, "Death is swallowed up in victory." And again, "For we know that if the earthly tent we live in is destroyed, we have a building from God, a house not made with hands, eternal in the heavens." Yes, again and again he defies the world to do its worst, believing that a better time is coming in the hereafter. I had two vivid reminders one time in Buffalo of how this hope of immortality saves the individual. On the day of my arrival there a tragic fire took the lives of a dozen or more little children. When one thinks of those frightened boys and girls frantically trying to escape from the flaming schoolroom, his heart breaks. And what could keep the minds of the grief-stricken parents from breaking if they had no hope of those little children being given another chance, somehow, somewhere? If innocent young lives could be cut off by causes beyond their control with no hope of fulfillment, this would be an insane world which would drive us insane.

Then on the last day of my stay in Buffalo my telephone rang. A woman called to say that she and her mother could not attend the cathedral where I was speaking. The mother had recently had her leg amputated. I expressed my sympathy and the hope that she would get around again before long. The daughter replied, "Well, you know mother is eighty-six. And she is ready to go. In fact, she is looking toward death rather eagerly as a great new experience." There is a woman wearing comfortably the helmet of hope which experience has fashioned.

But hope, as Paul interprets it, is more than the hope of salvation for the individual. It is the hope of salvation for God's work here as well as hereafter. Ah, we are beginning to wonder what hope there is of saving our world when now we read that one hydrogen bomb could be dropped to destroy a whole city like New York or Chicago. Does it not seem that the human race will go on perfecting its weapons until it commits suicide?

Personally I am vastly comforted by something which Albert Schweitzer said. He is considered by many as the world's greatest living man. Schweitzer tells us that he clings to a belief he gained in his youth. It is a belief in the power of truth to transcend all the force of circumstances. Nothing can permanently destroy truth. No lie lasts forever. But truth does. Therefore, Schweitzer is convinced that the race will not run the course of ruin right to the end.

The apostle Paul is in line with Schweitzer. Whatever comes, the ultimate values of truth, beauty, and goodness will go on. They are fireproof and bombproof. If these values are indestructible, then faith and hope and love can still abide. Therefore, said Paul, "Be steadfast, immovable, always abounding in the work of the Lord, knowing that in the Lord your labor is not in vain."

And the King, who was welcomed into Jerusalem nineteen centuries ago, will some day effect a final consummation of his kingdom and rule as King of kings and Lord of lords.

PRAYER:

Almighty God, whose most gracious Son rode into a city which hailed him and then rejected him, grant that his spirit may find lasting welcome in our loving hearts. Forgive us for the love of self which keeps us from following the highest roads of duty. Free us from the false pride of race or class which puts barriers across the path of peace and brotherhood. Open the minds of those who sit in darkness of their own making and unlock the hearts of those who have closed the gates of forgiveness. As we draw nearer to the cross, may we be filled with unbounded gratitude for the love given for us and may the angry passions of our bitter world give way to sympathy for all thy suffering children. O God, lead us in the way of peace. We ask through Jesus Christ our Lord. Amen.

CHAPTER VII

The Sword of the Spirit

THE LAST PIECE OF THE CHRISTIAN SOLDIER'S
equipment is "the sword of the Spirit, which is the word of
God."

The first five parts of the armor are for the protection
of the wearer. The girdle of truth, the breastplate of righteousness, the sandals of peace, the shield of faith, the helmet
of hope—all these are designed for defense. But the sword is
a weapon also for offensive action. The Christian is called not
only to withstand evil, but also to fight for the good.

Let us see, then, how the sword of the Spirit supple-
ments the other pieces of armor. First of all, it is the Christian's weapon in the fight for *truth*. The Apostle bade us
have our "loins [girt] with truth." That was the first direction
he gave. Truth is basic, and the search for truth is a task which
often costs a struggle.

When John Bunyan depicted the character which he
called "Ignorance," he made him say: "I think my heart is as
good as anybody's heart, and as for my thoughts, I take no
notice of them." Ignorance's attitude is all too much like many
of us. We think our heart is right because we have not really
studied our thoughts. The follower of Christ must search his
thoughts until he really knows his own mind. For this he needs
the sword of the Spirit, which is the word of God. Recall what
the Epistle to the Hebrews says: "The word of God is living
and active, sharper than any two-edged sword, piercing to the

69

division of soul and spirit, . . . and discerning the thoughts and intentions of the heart."

When the scripture speaks of the word of God, it does not mean merely the Bible which lies on our living-room tables. It means the living words of God which came to the men who wrote the Bible and can still come to you and me when we are sufficiently attuned to the Holy Spirit. And when we lazily and easily feel that our hearts are right, we need to listen intently to hear God's voice. He will waken us to discover our weakness. He will cut like a sword through the film of wishful thinking and lay bare our real motives. God will cleanse from the lens of our vision the prejudice and bias which prevent us from seeing the truth when it is presented to us. He will purge us of double-mindedness so that with purity of heart we shall see God in the midst of ungodliness.

We have to fight in order to free our own minds from error and inertia. And having done that, we are to become witnesses of truth to others. When Jesus stood before Pilate, Pilate asked him, "Are you the King of the Jews?" Jesus answered, "My kingship is not of this world." Then he went on to say: "For this I was born, and for this I have come into the world, to bear witness to the truth. Every one who is of the truth hears my voice."

The follower of Christ must first become one who rings true—true enough to vibrate to the truth as it was voiced by Christ. And then like his Lord he must go forth to bear witness to the truth. That means he must inform himself to the best of his ability on issues that matter. He must come to some vital conclusions and then stand for his convictions. Not arguing to prove himself right, but discussing to see what is right, he is to speak the truth in love and thus "grow up . . . into him who is the head, into Christ."

Something like this is involved when we take the sword of the Spirit and become fighters for truth.

Secondly, the sword of the Spirit enables us to fight for *righteousness*. Of course we need the breastplate of righteousness to protect us from the evils and temptations which beset us. But negative goodness is not good enough.

Outside Trinity Church in Boston stands St. Gaudens' statue of Phillips Brooks, the great preacher who made that parish famous. Just above and behind the stalwart form of Brooks the artist has placed the figure of Christ. One implication of the statue is clear. The noble minister was overshadowed, directed, and sustained by the Christ. It was that higher loyalty which held Brooks steady and unscathed amid the tumult and temptations of city life. But is there not also another implication of that statue, namely, that wherever Brooks went, he took the Christ with him? It was long remembered how Phillips Brooks radiated the spirit of Christ into darkened lives and situations in the city of Boston. Christ not only protects us; we are to project him.

I know a lady with some little grandchildren who have inherited a love of circuses. So once a year I sacrifice myself and take an afternoon off and help that grandmother take these little ones to the circus. There I watch the tightrope walkers as they balance themselves high above the crowd. Some people are like those circus acrobats. They can walk the taut line of the Ten Commandments without actually falling off. But they do not carry much weight. Christians are not meant to be moral acrobats. Christ would have us be moral athletes, who carry our virtues with such easy grace that we make goodness attractive to others and also help to "bear one another's burdens, and so fulfil the law of Christ."

Remember the Pharisee who thanked God that he was not as other men are, unjust, extortioners, adulterers. To be sure, that was good. But not good enough. Jesus said, "Unless your righteousness exceeds that of the scribes and Pharisees, you will never enter the kingdom of heaven." It is not enough for me to refrain from injustice. What am I doing to fight for justice and righteousness in my community and nation? It is not enough for me to be sexually pure. What am I doing to improve the morals of youth and strengthen the fidelity of families? In a time when righteousness is fighting such a tough battle with evil on so many fronts, can I be a follower of Christ and stay out of the fight?

This is the question which confronts the man outside the church. Some of the most personally upright people whom I know do not belong to the church. Perhaps they have not found a church with whose teachings they can agree. Perhaps they do not feel the need of the church to keep up their morale and their morals. They seem as virtuous as the persons who belong to the church. But the church with all its defects is the world's most potential organization for good. It offers the longest lever of helpfulness. It helps Christians to do together what they cannot do alone. The question, therefore, is: Can one render his largest service as a soldier of Christ if he does not join Christ's army? When we take the sword of the spirit, we are impelled to use the best we have for the highest we know in the fight for righteousness.

In the third place, the sword of the Spirit helps us to fight for *peace*. The sandals of peace are included in the armor of God. There is no word more welcome to our ears than the word "peace." How eagerly we read anything that offers peace of mind! How calming to our ears is the prayer of Whittier:

> Drop Thy still dews of quietness,
>   Till all our strivings cease;
> Take from our souls the strain and stress,
> And let our ordered lives confess
>   The beauty of Thy peace.

Drop into some church as you go about the noisy streets. Let the spell of its quietness steal over your rushing spirit. Look at the cross on the altar and let your thoughts run back to the Christ who reached out his arms to the restless throngs saying, "Come to me, all who labor and are heavy-laden, and I will give you rest." You begin to feel peace coming into your heart, don't you?

But keep looking at the cross. Think of the breadth and length and depth and height of the love revealed on that cross. And do you not begin to be disturbed by the awareness of your own shortcomings? Does not the sense of Christ's goodness stab you with a poignant penitence? Do you not begin to understand why Christ said, "I have not come to bring peace, but a sword"? When we catch the sympathy of Christ, we start to share the sufferings of Christ. The follower of Christ is not content with the shallow peace of mind which comes from comfortable adjustment to easy circumstances. He fights his way through laziness and selfishness to the peace of God which passes worldly understanding. On the last night of his earthly life, Jesus said: "Peace I leave with you; my peace I give to you; not as the world gives do I give to you." A person has to fight with the sword of the Spirit to attain a peace like that which can keep him when the cross awaits on the morrow.

And how we need "the sword of the Spirit, which is the word of God," to fight for peace in the international realm! The world is suffering today because it has too many watchers for war and too few workers for peace. We have been alerted to the point of hypertension. Many seem to feel that the only thing left now standing between us and a hot war is the new hydrogen bomb. Now is the time for the church to help men keep their heads and also use their heads.

Because the dangers of our day are very real, we need watchmen who scan horizons beyond the vision of the street.

But we must beware of irresponsible watchmen, for they deceive us with a false security. And emotional watchmen are a menace, for they excite us without real cause. And prejudiced watchmen are a peril, for they distort dangers and arouse us in wrong directions. The public guardians of our peace must not be blinded by fear or by the spotlight of publicity. They must not be mere head-hunters out to get somebody or mere headline hunters out to advance themselves. They must be persons who listen for a divine Voice above the cries of rival parties, who keep calm amid the excited clamor of the crowd, who have their eyes on the ultimate values rather than on the advantages of the moment. Such are the persons who wield the sword of the Spirit, which is the word of God.

History does not give us too much warrant in thinking that nations can be scared into peace. Years ago Hudson Maxim believed he had invented a gun so dangerous that nations would never again risk war. But they did. It would seem that no sane nation would now risk war when hydrogen bombs could wipe out a good-sized nation in a single night. Thomas Edison once predicted that there would one day spring from the brain of science a force so fearful that man would abandon war forever. And he expressed his faith that "what man's mind can create, man's character can control." But can we be sure? Not if man's motive is merely fear. Fear may fuse individuals and nations into blocs but not into brotherhood.

When we look at the leaders in the Kremlin, we see how empty their past promises have proved; and we feel how much further we have gone in our efforts for peace than have those wily diplomats. But when we look at the cross, do we feel that we have gone as far as the One who hung there would have us go? I for one do not believe that we have exhausted all the resources of goodwill in our efforts for peace. Let us take our patterns from the cross rather than from the

Kremlin. Let us show the peoples of other lands that we are truly interested in their welfare, their children, their health, their liberties. If we are sincerely out to help the needy nations, they will some day wake up to the fact. The truth will *out* for God is still *in*. That is what the soldier of Christ realizes when he takes the sword of the Spirit, which is the word of God.

In the fourth place, the sword of the Spirit helps us to fight for *faith*. The Christian is to put on the shield of faith which offers protection from so many of life's ills and evils. We are being repeatedly told that faith can shield us from futile anxieties and needless pains. But Christian faith is not content with mere self-protection.

On a visit to Charleston, South Carolina, I was taken into a very historic Presbyterian church. On the wall I saw a tablet in memory of a distinguished physician who lived some two hundred years ago. The inscription said that he was "constitutionally a valetudinarian." I wonder how many people know what that means. Frankly, I did not! I had the very humbling experience of having to be enlightened by a Presbyterian minister. That was very trying to a Methodist. But the Presbyterian pastor told me that he had not known it until he was told. Well, a valetudinarian is a person of very frail health. And yet that man despite his weak constitution lived a long life, and what is more, he was given strength to render strenuous and remarkable service as a doctor in the city. His faith helped him to fight not only for his own health but for the health of others.

Such is the true use of Christian faith. It is more than a shield for our own protection. It is a sword for use to help others in the struggle of life. I am greatly heartened to learn from time to time how many Christian Science friends listen to my radio addresses. One of them told me how she tried to instill in her children the truth that God's healing and helping power is given only to those who seek it for unselfish uses.

Some years ago in James Hilton's book *Random Harvest* an English clergyman was talking to a young couple about the struggle then threatening England. He said: "The time may come when it won't be enough to love England as a tired businessman loves his nap after lunch." We might paraphrase Hilton's words and say, "The time has come when it is not enough to love the kingdom of God as a tired businessman loves his nap after lunch." The time is here and now when we must "seek *first* his kingdom and his righteousness."

An English writer once gave a devastating description of a former British prime minister. He published a photograph of the political leader in his early years, with his lean, ascetic face and his flashing prophetic eye. Then on the next page he showed a picture of the man in his later years, heavy of jowl, dull of eye, his whole countenance suggesting smug complacency. The writer's comment was to ask whether we could expect the person of the second portrait to undertake anything heroic for the kingdom of God. Think how the vicious circles of war and injustice could be checked if the adventurous zeal of youth could be retained by men when they reach mature years and come into control of business and politics—yes, and of the church.

When the issues of peace and war, of the world's life and death, are in such delicate balance that one false move or rash gesture might tip the scales toward hell, let us take "the sword of the Spirit, which is the word of God," and line up on the side of faith.

And lastly the sword of the Spirit helps us to fight for and with *hope*. The Christian is bidden to put on the helmet of hope. But hope is a weapon as well as a protection.

Let me quote from a sermon which I gave over the

radio on March 22, 1945. If you remember, we were then in the closing days of World War II. D day had been passed. V day had not yet come. In my sermon I said: "When Britain will officially declare V day, we do not yet know. But the reality of victory came when Winston Churchill voiced the spirit that they would win though they had to fight on the beaches, on the streets, and in the fields."

The hour of real victory is not when the public finally acclaims the achievement but when the fighter becomes confident of victory in his own heart.

Recall the hour in which our national anthem was written. In 1814 during the British bombardment of Baltimore young Francis Scott Key went under a flag of truce aboard an English man-of-war. He was detained aboard the enemy ship while the fleet was firing on Fort McHenry. He watched the progress of the fight during the night, and in the morning, seeing the stars and stripes still flying, he composed the song "The Star-Spangled Banner." In it is the line: "Then conquer we must, when our cause it is just." Those words seemed foolishly optimistic at the time, for the chances seemed pretty slim that this little fledgling republic could win over the mighty British Empire.

Yet such is the way of hope. Victory is won in the mind and heart before it becomes visible to the public. So it is in the Christian's struggle. The little company of early Christians looked pitifully weak in contrast to the forces arrayed against them. What chance had the poor followers of a crucified Carpenter against the proud legions of an enthroned Caesar? Yet with the odds against them their Leader says:

"Fear not, little flock, for it is your Father's good pleasure to give you the kingdom." And back comes the antiphonal: "This is the victory that overcomes the world, our faith."

77

PRAYER:

Our Father, in whose light we find our leading and in whose mercy we have our hope, our hearts are filled with gratitude for thy goodness. For the liberties we enjoy, for the families and friendships which enrich our lives, for the laughter of little children and the ripened wisdom of the aging, we give thee hearty thanks. Take from us the tedious anxieties of the selfish mind and the weakness of the inconstant will. Defend us from the evils which attack us and make us strong to overcome evil with good. Grant that true learning, honest industry, and sound piety may abound among us. Guard and guide our homes and churches, our schools and colleges. Make thy presence felt, that bitterness may give way to brotherhood. O God, keep us from war and speed the day of peace. Through Jesus Christ our Lord. Amen.